W9-BHJ-157

I didn't know that tidal waves wash away cities

© Aladdin Books Ltd 1999
Produced by
Aladdin Books Ltd
28 Percy Street
London W1P 0LD

First published in the United States in 1999 by
Copper Beech Books,
an imprint of
The Millbrook Press
2 Old New Milford Road
Brookfield, Connecticut 06804

Concept, editorial, and design by
David West Children's Books

Designer: Flick Killerby
Illustrators: Peter Roberts – Allied Artists,
Jo Moore

Printed in Belgium

ISBN 0-7613-0922-5 (lib.bdg.)
ISBN 0-7613-0799-0 (trade)

5 4 3 2 1

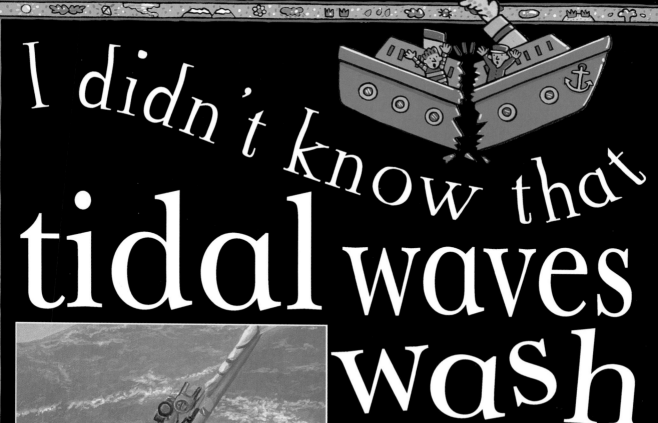

I didn't know that
tidal waves wash away cities

Kate Petty

COPPER BEECH BOOKS

BROOKFIELD, CONNECTICUT

I didn't know that

Introduction

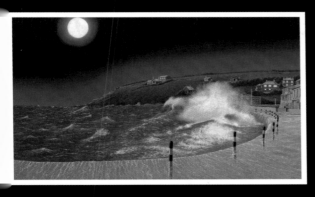

Did *you* know that most tidal waves are started by earthquakes? ... that the moon moves water? ... that the correct name for a tidal wave is a tsunami? ... that the sea can light up a town?

Discover for yourself amazing facts about tidal waves: how they start, the power they generate – and the havoc they can cause.

Watch for this symbol, which means there is a fun project for you to try.

Is it true or is it false? Watch for this symbol and try to answer the question before reading on for the answer.

True or false?
A tidal wave is caused by high tides.

Answer: **False**
Usually an earthquake or volcano is the cause of a tidal wave. Despite its name, a tidal wave has nothing to do with tides.

When an underwater earthquake cracks the seabed, huge pressure pushes the water above into waves. At sea the waves are far apart, but they get closer and higher as they reach the shore.

I didn't know that

tidal waves wash away cities. A 53-foot-high tidal wave swamped the people of Lisbon, Portugal, as they fled from falling, burning buildings in the earthquake of 1755, which killed 60,000 people.

6

The ancient Greek philosopher Plato described a perfect city called Atlantis that disappeared under the Mediterranean Sea. It might have been engulfed by a tidal wave, or it might have simply slipped into the sea.

The biggest ever tidal wave was 295 feet; taller than a skyscraper!

I didn't know that

volcanoes can set off *tsunamis*.
When Krakatoa in Indonesia blew its top in 1883 the explosion was heard 3,107 miles away. The volcano caused tsunamis that killed 37,000 people on the nearby islands of Java and Sumatra.

 True or false?

There are more than 10,000 volcanoes under the Pacific Ocean.

Answer: **True**
Part of the Pacific Ocean is called the "ring of fire" because it has thousands of underwater volcanoes (left) and 90% of tsunamis occur here.

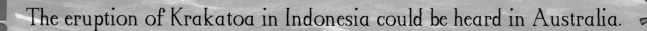
The eruption of Krakatoa in Indonesia could be heard in Australia.

Tsunami is the correct word for what we call tidal waves. It means "harbor wave" in Japanese. These waves are set off by earthquakes and volcanoes.

Where plates pull apart, magma rises and forms an ocean ridge.

Volcanoes form where two ocean plates meet.

The earth's *crust* is covered in *plates*. Where two ocean plates meet, one is forced down into the heat of the earth's *mantle* and may melt into *magma*, which can erupt as a volcano.

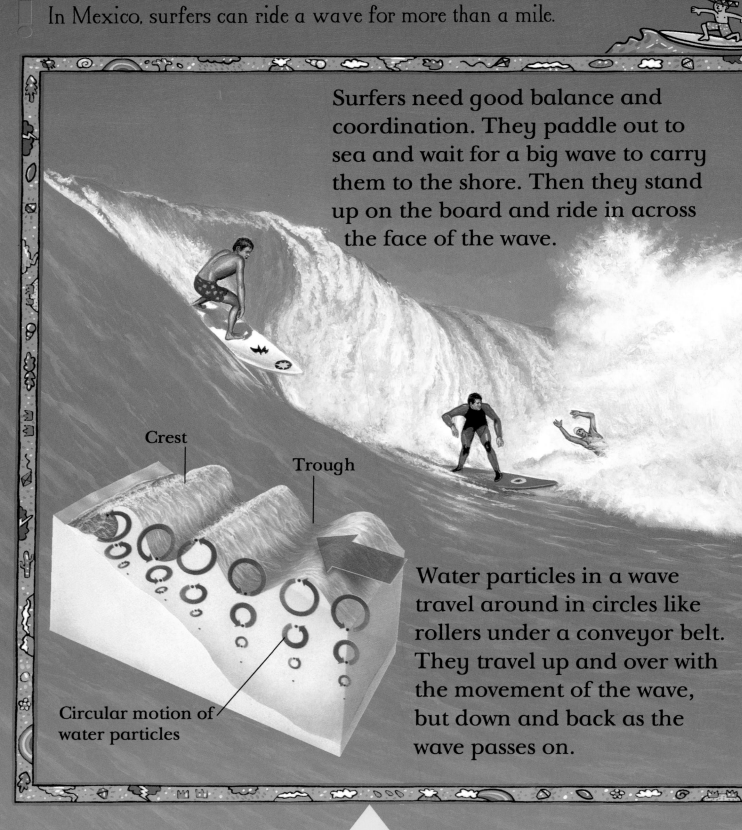

Surfers need good balance and coordination. They paddle out to sea and wait for a big wave to carry them to the shore. Then they stand up on the board and ride in across the face of the wave.

Crest

Trough

Water particles in a wave travel around in circles like rollers under a conveyor belt. They travel up and over with the movement of the wave, but down and back as the wave passes on.

Circular motion of water particles

I didn't know that

the sea stays still as the waves move forward. The water in a wave moves in circles. The wave is pushed forward by the wind and the movement of the water within it, but the sea itself stays in the same place.

SEARCH & FIND
Can you find three surfers?

Strong winds blow for great distances over the open sea, causing *swells* that can travel for thousands of miles. The rough seas seem to appear from nowhere – "out of the blue."

The highest wave ever ridden was almost 64 feet high.

I didn't know that

the moon moves water

because it causes tides. Tides happen because the *gravity* of the sun and the moon pull on the earth's oceans, causing the water to rise and fall as the world spins.

This coast road in Holland is built on land that was once under the sea. High *dikes* hold back the sea.

Extra high "spring" tides occur when the sun and the moon are in line and both pulling in the same direction. Lower "neap" tides occur when the sun and moon are pulling in different directions.

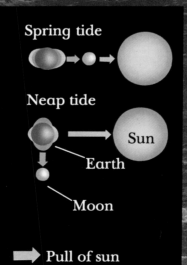

Spring tide

Neap tide

Sun

Earth

Moon

Pull of sun
Pull of moon

A Dutch story tells of a boy who plugged a hole in a dike with his finger.

The Thames River is affected by the tides. The Thames Barrier at Woolwich (left) was built to protect London from flooding during exceptionally high tides.

SEARCH & FIND

Can you find four lit houses?

FIND & SEARCH

13

I didn't know that

waves can break a ship in two. *Tropical storms* at sea can strike suddenly with mountainous waves. Old wooden ships stood little chance, but even modern boats can be wrecked in stormy seas.

One of the most dangerous places in the world is Cape Horn at the very tip of South America. Sailors have always feared the dangerous conditions and the icy waters there.

A ship's computerized weather maps predict stormy weather that occurs when a warm front (round symbols) meets a cold front (triangles.)

Lighthouses warn sailors away from rocky shores at night. Make your own lighthouse from a cardboard tube. Cut out windows and paint it with stripes. Stand a flashlight inside and put a cardboard lid on top. Complete the scene with a papier mâché rock and modeling clay boats.

Cape Horn has more shipwrecks than anywhere else.

I didn't know that

a storm at sea can come ashore. Huge waves whipped up by a hurricane at sea can come ashore ahead of the storm itself. Ships end up stranded hundreds of yards from the coastline.

True or false?
Hurricane and typhoon are both names for tropical storms.

Answer: **True**
Hurricane comes from the Carib word *huracan*, meaning "evil spirit." Typhoon comes from the Chinese *tai fung*, meaning "big wind."

Hurricane

Storm surge

When huge waves come ashore ahead of the storm it is called a storm surge.

A storm surge can raise the level of the sea by 20 feet. Flooding after a tropical storm in Bangladesh in 1991 killed 250,000 people and left millions without their homes, animals, or possessions.

A hurricane can move at the speed of a car down a highway.

I didn't know that

a tsunami could destroy a whole village. In 1992, two thousand villagers were killed when a tsunami, 85 feet high, crashed into their fragile wooden homes in Flores, Indonesia, causing devastation.

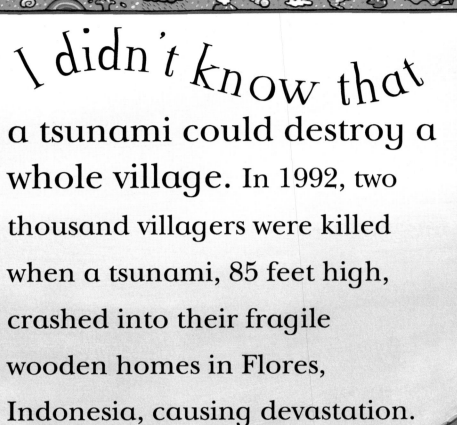

 True or false?
People at sea don't notice tsunamis.

Answer: **True**
In 1896, Japanese fishermen had no idea that one of the waves beneath their boats went on to kill 27,000 people back home.

In 1998, islanders settling down for the evening in Papua New Guinea were caught off-guard by three 49-foot tsunamis, set off by an earthquake 12 miles out to sea. More than 2,000 people died. These survivors came back to find their homes had been wrecked.

In 1960, a tsunami in Chile killed more than 1,000 people and destroyed 50,000 homes. Fourteen hours later it slammed into Hilo, Hawaii, killing an additional 61 people.

Alaska

Hawaii

Isla de Chiloe
Chile

A tsunami can move as fast as a jet airplane.

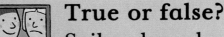

Helicopters are useful in sea rescues because they can hover while a survivor is winched to safety. They use radar and infrared scanners to pinpoint people in the sea.

True or false?
Sailors have been known to survive for several days after capsizing in cold waters.

Answer: **True**
In January, 1997, around-the-world yachtsman Tony Bullimore spent five days under his overturned 60-foot yacht before being rescued 1,300 miles south of Australia.

The sea can be a dangerous place. Wearing a life jacket could save your life. Never go sailing without telling someone where you are going and when you expect to be back.

I didn't know that

some boats are unsinkable. Modern lifeboats have the power to skim over the tops of very high waves. They are also designed to right themselves if they keel over. Satellite links help them to locate a ship in trouble.

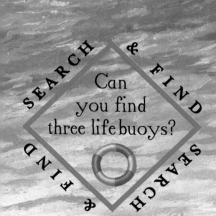

SEARCH & FIND & FIND & SEARCH

Can you find three life buoys?

❗ Two fishermen were adrift for 177 days after a cyclone hit.

Families who live in tsunami areas need an *evacuation* plan and an emergency kit on hand. The kit should contain: a flashlight and extra batteries, a portable battery radio, a first-aid kit with medicines, emergency food and water, a can opener, money, and sturdy shoes.

Eyewitnesses to tsunamis describe the way the sea first pulls back with a hissing, sucking sound, rather like the noise of a jet engine, before it rears up in a huge, engulfing wave. The rumble of a nearby earthquake is another warning sign.

Tsunamis can be caused by meteorites landing in the sea.

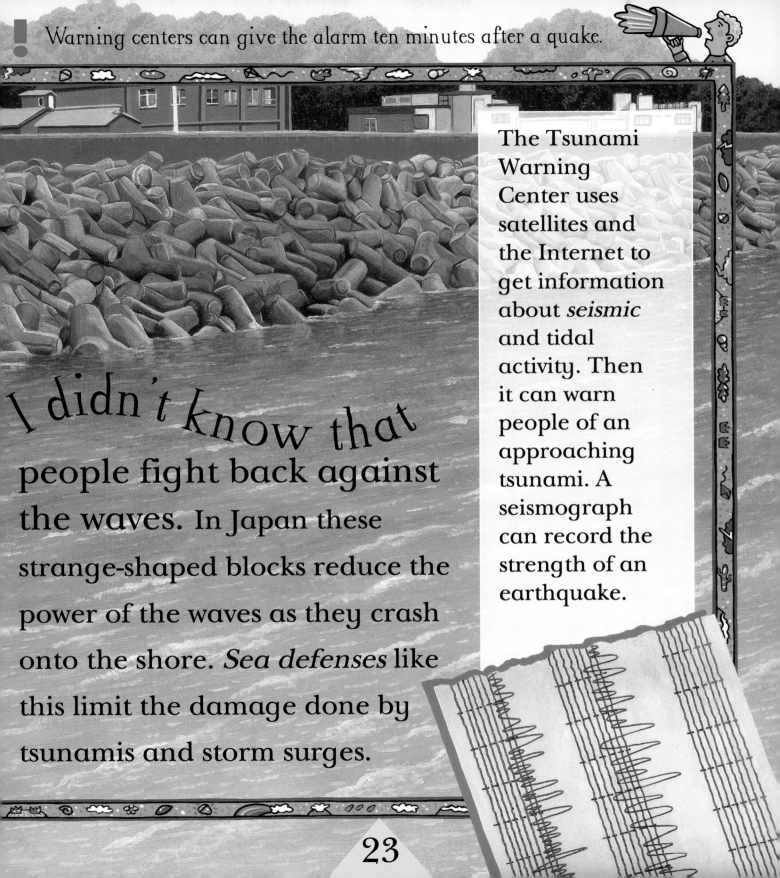

The Tsunami Warning Center uses satellites and the Internet to get information about *seismic* and tidal activity. Then it can warn people of an approaching tsunami. A seismograph can record the strength of an earthquake.

I didn't know that people fight back against the waves. In Japan these strange-shaped blocks reduce the power of the waves as they crash onto the shore. *Sea defenses* like this limit the damage done by tsunamis and storm surges.

"St. Elmo's fire" can sometimes be seen around the mast of a ship in stormy seas. It occurs when the moving air inside a storm cloud builds up static electricity, which gathers around the highest point of the ship, the mast.

Waterspouts are an awe-inspiring sight, but fortunately they are rarely dangerous. They usually last about 15 minutes. Most waterspouts are only 16 to 32 feet thick and between 164 and 328 feet high.

I didn't know that

the sea can be sucked up into the sky. A waterspout is a *tornado* at sea. When rapidly rising warm air meets falling cool air, it sets up a spinning funnel, which sucks up the water from the surface of the sea.

 True or false?
Sometimes one waterspout can follow after another.

Answer: **True**
At Martha's Vineyard (off the southeast coast of Massachusetts) in 1896, there were three waterspouts within just 45 minutes.

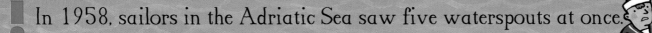 In 1958, sailors in the Adriatic Sea saw five waterspouts at once.

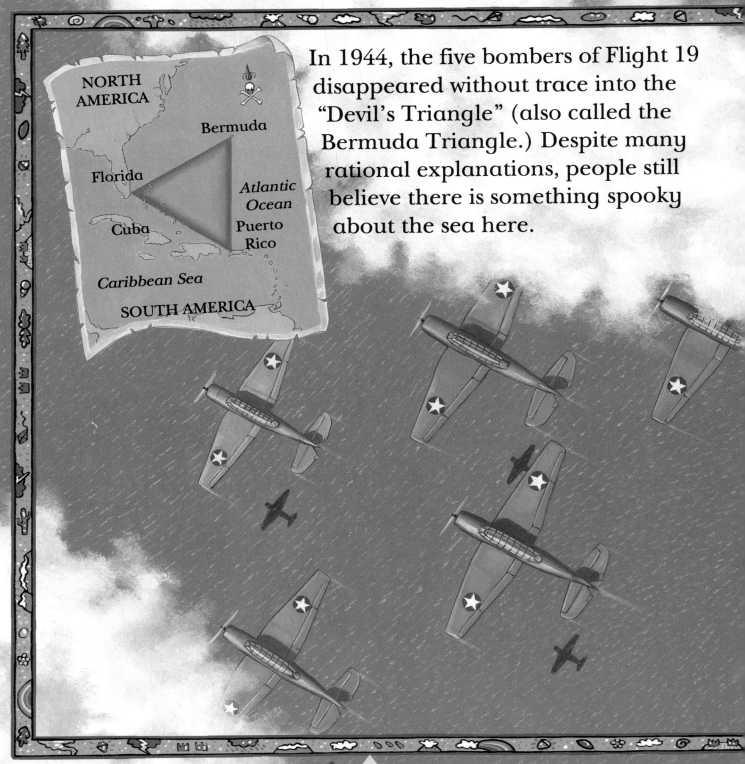

NORTH AMERICA

Bermuda

Florida

Atlantic Ocean

Cuba

Puerto Rico

Caribbean Sea

SOUTH AMERICA

In 1944, the five bombers of Flight 19 disappeared without trace into the "Devil's Triangle" (also called the Bermuda Triangle.) Despite many rational explanations, people still believe there is something spooky about the sea here.

I didn't know that

there are still unsolved mysteries of the sea. More than 70 ships and 20 planes have been lost in the "Bermuda Triangle," maybe because this stormy area of the Atlantic Ocean has undersea earthquakes and volcanoes as well as awkward *currents.*

 True or false?
El Niño can cause flooding in the desert.

Answer: **True**
In 1983, El Niño brought high winds and flooding to the Arizona desert. It can cause strange weather, like snow in places that are usually hot or drought in wet places. It can also often bring violent weather.

"El Niño" is the movement of warm water in the Pacific, eastward from Indonesia toward the Americas.

America

Warm water

El Niño can cause flowers to bloom in the desert.

I didn't know that

the sea can light up a town. Using the power of waves and tides is not a new idea. However, there are experimental systems now, that have shown that they can provide large amounts of electricity.

The Osprey 2000 wave system can operate near the shore.

28

Run a faucet onto a toy waterwheel and see how the power of the water turns the wheel. The turning of the wheel produces energy. You can make a waterwheel with a spool that can spin on a pencil.

Wave power is a way of generating electricity. One day it should be possible to harness the power of strong, deep water waves out at sea.

The biggest waterpower plant is ITAIPU. Built by Brazil and Paraguay, it supplies a quarter of Brazil's electricity and more than three quarters of Paraguay's.

Tide-powered water mills have been used for thousands of years.

Glossary

Crust
The hard, rocky outer layer of the earth's surface.

Currents
Movement of water in the oceans set up by the winds, water temperatures, and the spin of the world.

Dike
A wall that holds back water.

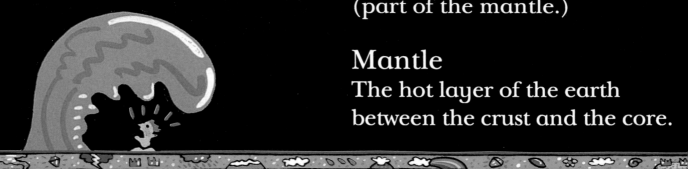

Evacuation
Clearing people from a dangerous building or place.

Gravity
A force that "pulls" objects toward each other like an apple falling to the earth.

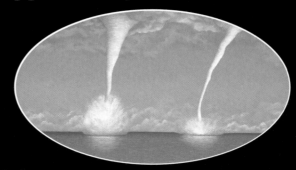

Magma
The layer of molten rock beneath the earth's surface (part of the mantle.)

Mantle
The hot layer of the earth between the crust and the core.

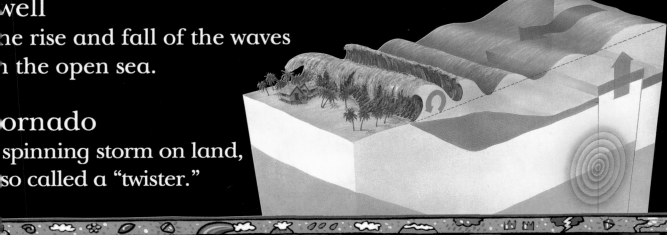

ates

he earth's crust is divided
to about 15 plates that are
ways moving on the liquid
rface of the magma below.

ea defenses

ny way of protecting land
om the power of the sea.

eismic

o do with earthquakes
eism is another word for
rthquake.)

well

he rise and fall of the waves
the open sea.

ornado

spinning storm on land,
so called a "twister."

Tropical storm

Violent storms, with high-
speed winds, that form over
tropical seas in very warm
weather. Called hurricanes,
typhoons, or cyclones,
depending on where
they are.

Tsunami

Giant wave caused by an
earthquake or volcano, a
better word for "tidal wave."

Index

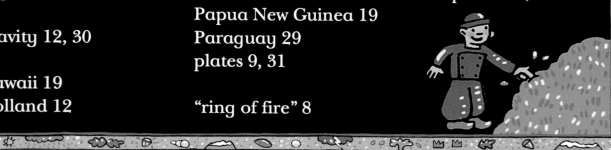